TABLE OF
CONTENTS

Introduction

- Brief overview of the book's content and purpose
- Target audience: beginners looking to start an Etsy shop

Chapter 1: Understanding the Etsy Platform

- Overview of the Etsy platform and its features
- Setting up an Etsy account and creating a shop
- Navigating the Etsy interface and tools

Aim: to provide a comprehensive understanding of the Etsy platform for beginners

Chapter 2: Optimizing Your Online Store

- Importance of product photography and how to take high-quality photos
- Tips for creating effective product descriptions
- Strategies for pricing and shipping

Aim: to help beginners create an attractive and user-friendly online store

Chapter 3: Attracting Customers

- Importance of marketing and how to promote your store
- Strategies for building a following and increasing visibility
- Tips for networking and collaborating with other Etsy sellers

Aim: to help beginners attract customers to their store

Chapter 4: Managing Your Time and Inventory

- Tips for managing time effectively and balancing multiple tasks
- Strategies for finding suppliers and maintaining inventory

Aim: to help beginners manage their time and inventory efficiently

Chapter 5: Understanding Legal Requirements

- Overview of legal requirements for operating an online store
- Tips for complying with taxes and regulations

Aim: to help beginners understand and comply with legal requirements

Introduction: Starting an Etsy Shop - A Journey of Empowerment and Creativity

Starting an Etsy shop is a journey of empowerment and creativity. It's an opportunity to turn your passion into a business and share your unique creations with the world. However, it's also a journey that can be filled with uncertainty and fear. The process can be overwhelming, and it's easy to feel lost and alone. But let us assure you, that you are not alone in this journey, and with the right resources and support, you can navigate the Etsy platform, create a successful online store, and attract customers.

This book is your guide to starting an Etsy shop. It's designed to provide you with the knowledge and skills you need to navigate the Etsy platform and create a successful online store. It's written for beginners, like you, who may not have experience with e-commerce or online sales. With this book,you will learn how to set up and optimize your shop, how to market your products, and how to stay compliant with legal requirements.

As you read through this book, you will feel a sense of empowerment as you gain the knowledge and skills you need to create a successful online store. You will learn how to take high-quality product photos, how to create effective product descriptions, and how to price and ship your products. You will also learn how to market your products and attract customers to your store. You will feel a sense of pride as you see your online store come to life and see your products being sold.

However, starting an Etsy shop can also be a journey of uncertainty and fear. You may feel overwhelmed by the process and uncertain about whether you have what it takes to succeed. You may feel a sense of fear as you wonder whether you will be able to attract customers and make a profit. But with the right resources and support, you can overcome these obstacles and turn your dream of starting an Etsy shop into a reality. Starting an Etsy shop is a journey of empowerment and creativity.

with legal requirements.

As you read through this book, you will feel a sense of empowerment as you gain the knowledge and skills you need to create a successful online store. You will learn how to take high-quality product photos, how to create effective product descriptions, and how to price and ship your products. You will also learn how to market your products and attract customers to your store. You will feel a sense of pride as you see your online store come to life and see your products being sold.

However, starting an Etsy shop can also be a journey of uncertainty and fear. You may feel overwhelmed by the process and uncertain about whether you have what it takes to succeed. You may feel a sense of fear as you wonder whether you will be able to attract customers and make a profit. But with the right resources and support, you can overcome these obstacles and turn your dream of starting an Etsy shop into a reality.This book is not only a guide but also a companion.. It's here to support you as you navigate the Etsy platform, create a successful online store, and attract customers. It's here to offer you the encouragement you need when you're feeling overwhelmed and the guidance you need when you're unsure of what to do next. It's here to remind you that you are not alone in this journey and that with the right resources and support, you can succeed.

Starting an Etsy shop is a journey of empowerment and creativity. It's an opportunity to turn your passion into a business and share your unique creations with the world. But it's also a journey that can be filled with uncertainty and fear. With this book as your guide, you will have the knowledge and skills you need to navigate the Etsy platform, create a successful online store, and attract customers. You will feel empowered as you gain the knowledge and skills you need to create a successful online store. With this guide, you will not only be able to create a successful online store but also overcome any fear or uncertainty that you may face along the way.

So, let's start this journey together and turn your passion into a business! Let's empower ourselves, and let's create something beautiful. This book is going to be your companion throughout this journey and it's going to help you turn your dream into a reality. Let's take the first step and make this happen.

Brief overview of the book's content and purpose

Starting an Etsy shop can be a daunting task, especially for beginners who may not have experience with e-commerce or online sales. The book "Understanding the Etsy Platform and Setting up an Online Store" is designed to empower and guide those who are ready to take the leap and start their own Etsy shop.

The book is filled with practical advice and actionable steps for navigating the Etsy platform, creating an attractive and user-friendly online store, and attracting customers. It is written with the beginner in mind and is designed to be easy to understand and follow.

The first chapter, "Understanding the Etsy Platform," delves into the features and tools available on the Etsy platform. It provides a comprehensive understanding of how to set up an account ,create a shop, and navigate the interface.This chapter is essential for beginners who may be intimidated by the platform and unsure of where to start.

The second chapter, "Optimizing Your Online Store," focuses on the importance of product photography and creating effective product descriptions. It provides tips and strategies for pricing and shipping, helping beginners create an online store that stands out and attracts customers. The emotional language used in this chapter, makes the readers feel like they are not alone in the process and they are capable of creating a beautiful online store.

The third chapter, "Attracting Customers," is all about marketing and promoting your store. It offers strategies for building a following and increasing visibility, as well as tips for networking and collaborating with other Etsy sellers. This chapter is designed to help beginners attract customers to their store and build a loyal following.

The fourth chapter, "Managing Your Time and Inventory," is all about time management and inventory. It offers tips for managing time effectively and balancing multiple tasks, as well as strategies for finding suppliers and maintaining inventory.

This chapter is designed to help beginners manage their time and inventory efficiently, so they can focus on creating and listing new products.

The fifth chapter, "Understanding Legal Requirements," provides an overview of legal requirements for operating an online store. It offers tips for complying with taxes and regulations and provides resources for further learning and support. This chapter is essential for beginners who may be intimidated by the legal requirements of operating an online store.

Overall, "Understanding the Etsy Platform and Setting up an Online Store" is a comprehensive guide for beginners who are ready to start their own Etsy shop. It is filled with practical advice, actionable steps, and emotional language, to help beginners navigate the Etsy platform, create an attractive online store, and attract customers.With this book as a guide, beginners can feel confident and empowered to start their own Etsy shop and turn their passion into a successful business.

Target audience: beginners looking to start an Etsy shop

Starting an Etsy shop can be an exciting, yet daunting task for beginners. The thought of turning your passion into a business and seeing your creations come to life can fill you with a sense of hope and purpose. However, the reality of setting up an online store, managing inventory, and attracting customers can also be overwhelming and scary. The good news is, with the right knowledge and guidance, starting an Etsy shop can be a fulfilling and profitable journey.

As a beginner looking to start an Etsy shop, you may be feeling a mix of emotions - excitement, uncertainty, and maybe even a little bit of fear. You may be thinking, "Will I be able to create a successful store? Will people like my products? Will I be able to make a profit?" These are natural thoughts and feelings to have, and they are all part of the process of starting a business. But, with the right tools and resources, you can turn your Etsy shop into a reality.One of the most important things to consider as a beginner is understanding the Etsy platform.. Etsy is a unique marketplace that allows you to sell handmade, vintage, and craft items. It's a platform that provides you with the tools and resources to create a professional-looking online store, and it's a great way to reach a global audience. However, it's also a platform that can be overwhelming for beginners. That's why it's essential to understand the features and tools available on Etsy, so you can make the most of the platform and set up a store that is optimized for success.

Once you have a grasp of the Etsy platform, the next step is to optimize your online store. This includes creating attractive and high-quality product photographs, writing effective product descriptions, and pricing your products competitively. These are all crucial elements of a successful Etsy store, and they will help you stand out from the competition. By investing the time and effort into creating a visually appealing and user-friendly store, you will be able to attract customers and increase your sales.

Attracting customers is another crucial aspect of starting an

Etsy shop. As a beginner, you may not have a large following or established reputation, which can make it challenging to attract customers. However, by using effective marketing strategies, such as social media promotion and networking with other Etsy sellers, you can increase your visibility and attract customers to your store.

Managing your time and inventory is also a key aspect of running a successful Etsy shop. As a beginner, it can be challenging to balance multiple tasks and manage your time effectively. However, by setting up a system for managing inventory and organizing your time, you can ensure that your store runs smoothly and efficiently.

Lastly, as a beginner, it's essential to understand the legal requirements for operating an online store. This includes taxes and regulations that must be complied with. Failure to comply with legal requirements can lead to penalties and fines, which can negatively impact your business. By understanding the legal requirements, you can ensure that your store is operating legally and ethically.

Starting an Etsy shop as a beginner can be a challenging and emotional journey. However, with the right knowledge and resources, you can turn your passion into a profitable business. By understanding the Etsy platform, optimizing your online store, attracting customers, managing your time and inventory, and understanding legal requirements, you can set yourself up for success. With determination and a bit of hard work, your Etsy shop can be the beginning of a fulfilling and profitable journey.

Chapter 1
Understanding the Etsy Platform

Starting an Etsy shop can be an exciting and fulfilling experience, but it can also be overwhelming and daunting. The Etsy platform is packed with features and tools that can be difficult to navigate, especially for beginners. However, understanding the Etsy platform is crucial to the success of your shop. In this chapter, we will explore the ins and outs of the Etsy platform and provide you with the knowledge and skills you need to set up and manage a successful shop.

When you first log into Etsy, you'll be greeted with a dashboard that can be overwhelming to navigate. However, with a little bit of practice and patience, you'll quickly become familiar with the different sections and features of the platform. From your dashboard, you'll be able to manage your listings, track your sales, and respond to customer inquiries. You'll also be able to access tools that will help you market and promote your shop, such as tags, keywords, and shop sections.

One of the most important sections of the Etsy platform is your shop settings. This is where you'll be able to customize your shop's appearance, set up payment and shipping options, and manage your billing and taxes. It's important to take the time to set up your shop settings correctly, as this will impact the overall functionality and appearance of your shop.

Another important feature of the Etsy platform is the ability to create and manage listings. This is where you'll be able to create and edit product listings, upload photos, and write product descriptions. Creating great listings is crucial to the success of your shop, as they will be the first thing that customers see when they visit your shop. Make sure to take the time to create detailed and accurate product descriptions, and upload high-quality photos that showcase your products in the best possible light.

Etsy also offers a variety of tools and resources to help you market and promote your shop. From tags and keywords to shop sections, these tools will help you reach a wider audience and increase your visibility on the platform.

Additionally, Etsy offers a variety of marketing and promotion options, such as paid advertising and featured listings, that will help you drive more traffic to your shop.

In conclusion, understanding the Etsy platform is essential to the success of your shop. It can be overwhelming and daunting, but with a little bit of patience and practice, you'll quickly become familiar with the features and tools of the platform. By mastering the Etsy platform, you'll be able to set up and manage a successful shop, attract customers, and drive sales. With a little bit of effort and determination, you'll be able to turn your passion into a profitable business.

Overview of the Etsy platform and its features

The Etsy platform is a treasure trove of creativity and uniqueness, bursting at the seams with one-of-a-kind products that are sure to delight and inspire. From handcrafted jewelry to vintage finds, the platform offers a vast selection of goods that are sure to capture the hearts of shoppers around the world.

As soon as you step into the world of Etsy, you'll be greeted with a vibrant and colorful display of products that are sure to make your heart skip a beat. The platform is a true feast for the senses, with an endless array of stunning goods that are sure to take your breath away. Whether you're looking for a unique piece of jewelry, a vintage piece of clothing, or a handmade item for your home, Etsy has something for everyone.

One of the most appealing features of the Etsy platform is the vast selection of goods that are available. From handcrafted jewelry to vintage finds, the platform offers a wide range of products that are sure to delight and inspire. The platform is a true melting pot of creativity, where artisans and creators from around the world come together to showcase their unique talents and creations.

The Etsy platform is also incredibly user-friendly, making it easy for shoppers to navigate and find the perfect item. The platform's search bar allows you to search for specific items or browse through different categories, making it easy to find exactly what you're looking for. And with the platform's easy-to-use filters, you can narrow down your search to find the perfect item that meets your specific needs.

One of the most exciting features of the Etsy platform is the ability for shoppers to connect with the creators of the products they're purchasing. Etsy allows shoppers to connect with artisans and creators, giving them the opportunity to learn more about the products they're buying, and even ask questions or request customizations. This creates a more personal and emotional connection between the shopper and the product, making the shopping experience even more special.

The Etsy platform is also incredibly supportive of its community of sellers, offering a range of tools and resources to help them grow their businesses. The platform offers a variety of marketing and advertising tools, as well as educational resources, to help sellers succeed on the platform. This supportive community helps new sellers to thrive and succeed, and it also creates a strong sense of camaraderie among sellers on the platform.

The Etsy platform is truly a magical place, where creativity and individuality come together to create a shopping experience that is truly one-of-a-kind. With its vast selection of unique and handcrafted goods, user-friendly interface, and supportive community, it's no wonder that shoppers around the world are falling in love with the Etsy platform. Whether you're a seasoned shopper or a newbie, the Etsy platform is sure to leave you feeling inspired, delighted, and maybe even a little bit in love.

Setting up an Etsy account and creating a shop

Starting an Etsy shop can be an exciting, yet overwhelming experience. The thought of creating your own online store and selling your unique products to the world is exhilarating. However, the process of setting up an Etsy account and creating a shop can be daunting for beginners. It's easy to get lost in the sea of information and feel overwhelmed by the technical details. But don't let that stop you from pursuing your dream of becoming an Etsy shop owner. With a little guidance and patience, you can easily set up an Etsy account and create a shop that will make your heart sing.

The first step in setting up an Etsy shop is to create an account. This is a simple process that requires you to provide your name, email address, and a password. Once you've created your account, you'll be taken to the Etsy homepage where you can start creating your shop. This is where the magic begins, and where you can unleash your creativity and make your shop truly unique.

When creating your shop, you'll be asked to choose a shop name and a shop location. This is your chance to make a lasting impression and stand out from the crowd. The shop name is the first thing that customers will see when they come across your shop, so it's important to choose something that is memorable and reflective of your brand. The shop location is also important as it will help customers find your shop when searching for products in your area.

Once you've chosen your shop name and location, you can start customizing your shop. This is where you can let your imagination run wild and create a shop that is truly one-of-a-kind. You can choose a custom banner, add your own logo, and select a color scheme that reflects your brand. You can also set up your shop policies, which will help customers understand your terms and conditions.

Once your shop is set up, it's time to start listing products. This is where the excitement truly begins as you showcase your unique products to the world.You can add product listings, photos, and descriptions, and set prices for your products. It's important to remember that the quality of your product photos is crucial as they are the first thing that customers will see when browsing your shop. Make sure that your photos are clear, well-lit, and showcase your products in the best possible light.

In conclusion, setting up an Etsy account and creating a shop may seem daunting at first, but it's a process that can be easily mastered with a little guidance and patience. It's an opportunity to unleash your creativity and make your shop truly unique. Remember to choose a shop name and location that reflects your brand, customize your shop, and showcase your products in the best possible light. With a little effort and determination, you'll be well on your way to creating a shop that will make your heart sing.

Navigating the Etsy interface and tools

Navigating the Etsy interface and tools can be a daunting task for beginners. The platform offers a wide range of features and tools that can be overwhelming to those who are new to the world of e-commerce. However, mastering these tools is essential to creating a successful Etsy shop.

The first step in navigating the Etsy interface is to set up an account and create a shop. This process can be nerve-wracking, as you may feel unsure of where to start and what information to include. However, Etsy provides clear instructions and prompts to guide you through the process. Once your shop is set up, you will be taken to the main dashboard, which serves as the hub for managing your store. The dashboard allows you to see important information such as your sales, traffic, and reviews. It also gives you access to various tools such as the listing manager, which allows you to create and manage your products. This tool can be a lifesaver for beginners who may not know how to create effective product descriptions and take high-quality photos. The listing manager also allows you to set your prices, shipping options and inventory.

Another important tool on the Etsy platform is the analytics tool. This tool provides valuable insights into how your store is performing and allows you to track your sales, traffic, and conversion rates. It can be a game-changer for beginners who may not know how to measure the success of their store. With this tool, you can see what's working and what's not and make adjustments accordingly.

Etsy also offers a range of marketing and promotion tools to help you reach a wider audience and increase visibility for your store. These tools include advertising options, social media integrations, and the ability to create coupons and discounts. The promotion tools are a treasure trove for beginners who may not know how to market their products effectively.

The Etsy platform also offers a range of communication tools, such as the ability to message customers and respond to reviews. This is a powerful tool that can help you build relationships with your customers and create a sense of trust and loyalty. It can also be a lifesaver for beginners who may not know how to handle customer complaints or issues.

In conclusion, the Etsy platform offers a wide range of features and tools that can be overwhelming for beginners. However, mastering these tools is essential to creating a successful Etsy shop. The platform provides clear instructions and prompts to guide you through the process and offers a range of tools that can help you create, manage, market and communicate with your customers. With time and practice, you will be able to navigate the Etsy interface and tools like a pro and take your Etsy shop to the next level.

Chapter 2
Optimizing Your Online Store

Welcome to the chapter on optimizing your online store! As a beginner Etsy shop owner, it's essential to understand the importance of creating an attractive and user-friendly online store that will draw customers in and make them want to purchase from you. In this chapter, we will go over some key strategies for optimizing your store, including product photography, creating effective product descriptions, and pricing and shipping.

When it comes to product photography, the first thing to keep in mind is that the photos are the first thing customers will see when they visit your shop. High-quality, well-lit product photos are essential for showcasing your products in the best possible light. They can make the difference between a customer clicking on your listing or passing it by. By taking the time to set up the scene, take multiple shots, and choose the best one, you'll be able to take great product photos that will help you drive sales and grow your business.

Creating effective product descriptions is another essential aspect of optimizing your online store. Your product descriptions should be clear and concise, and they should provide customers with all the information they need to make an informed purchase. You should also use descriptive language that evokes emotions and makes customers want to own the product. For example, if you're selling jewelry, your descriptions should make the customer feel glamorous and elegant. If you're selling home decor, your descriptions should make the customer feel cozy and comfortable.

Pricing and shipping are also important factors to consider when optimizing your online store. You'll want to make sure that your prices are competitive and that you're offering fair shipping rates. It's also important to be transparent about your shipping policies and to provide customers with detailed information about shipping times and costs. By doing this, you'll be able to build trust with your customers and ensure a positive shopping experience.

In conclusion, optimizing your online store is essential for driving sales and growing your Etsy shop. By understanding the importance of product photography, creating effective product descriptions, and pricing and shipping, you'll be able to create an attractive and user-friendly online store that will draw customers in and make them want to purchase from you. With a little bit of effort and practice, you'll be able to create an online store that will help you achieve your business goals and reach your full potential as an Etsy shop owner.

Importance of product photography and how to take high-quality photos

Product photography is one of the most crucial elements of setting up and running a successful Etsy shop. High-quality product photos are essential for attracting customers and showcasing your products in the best possible light. They can make the difference between a customer clicking on your listing or passing it by, and ultimately determine your sales success.

When a customer visits your shop, the first thing they will see is the product photos. They will use them to make a quick decision about whether or not to purchase from your shop. If your photos are poorly lit, blurry, or low-resolution, customers will have a hard time getting a sense of the product and will likely move on to a different shop. On the other hand, if your photos are crisp, clear, and well-lit, customers will be drawn in and will have a better understanding of the product and feel compelled to make a purchase.

Taking high-quality product photos is not just about having a good camera and knowing how to use it. It's also about understanding how to set up the scene and create an emotional connection with the customer. Product photography should evoke feelings in the customer and make them want to own the product. For example, if you're selling jewelry, your photos should make the customer feel glamorous and elegant. If you're selling home decor, your photos should make the customer feel cozy and comfortable.

One of the most important things to keep in mind when taking product photos is lighting. The best way to achieve great lighting is to shoot in natural light. This means using natural light sources such as windows or outdoor areas to illuminate your products. If you're shooting indoors, try to position your product near a window or skylight. Avoid using flash as it can create harsh shadows and make your product look unnatural.

Another important aspect of product photography is composition. You want to make sure that your product is the focal point of the photo and that the background is not distracting. Keep the background simple and neutral, and avoid clutter. You can also use props to add context and interest to the photo. For example, if you're selling a book, you can include a photo of someone reading it.

When it comes to editing your photos, keep it simple. You want to make sure that the colors are accurate and that the photo is well-exposed. Avoid over-editing as this can make the photo look unnatural. The best way to achieve great product photos is to take the time to set up the scene, take multiple shots, and choose the best one.

In conclusion, product photography is a vital aspect of running a successful Etsy shop. High-quality product photos can make the difference between a customer making a purchase or moving on to the next shop. By understanding how to take great product photos, you can create an emotional connection with your customers and showcase your products in the best possible light. With a little bit of effort and practice, you'll be able to take great product photos that will *help you drive sales and grow your business.*

Tips for creating effective product descriptions

Creating effective product descriptions is essential for any Etsy shop owner looking to attract customers and boost sales. Your product descriptions are the first thing potential customers will see when browsing your store, and they play a crucial role in convincing them to make a purchase. To help you create compelling and effective product descriptions, here are some tips to keep in mind.

First, focus on the emotional appeal of your product. People buy things because of the way they make them feel, not just because of their practical uses. Use vivid and descriptive language to evoke emotions and create a sense of desire in your customers. For example, instead of describing a candle as "scented," describe it as "a warm, cozy aroma that fills the room with a sense of home."

Next, highlight the unique features of your product. What sets it apart from similar products on the market? Use specific, detailed language to communicate the benefits of your product and why it's worth purchasing. For example, instead of describing a piece of jewelry as "handmade," describe it as "a one-of-a-kind, handmade piece crafted with care and attention to detail."

Third, use persuasive language to encourage customers to make a purchase. Use words like "limited," "exclusive," and "discounted" to create a sense of urgency and encourage customers to act fast.

Finally, keep your product descriptions concise and to the point. People have short attention spans, and they don't want to read a long-winded description. Keep your descriptions short and sweet, and use bullet points to break up the text and make it more readable.

In conclusion, creating effective product descriptions is essential for any Etsy shop owner looking to attract customers and boost sales. By focusing on the emotional appeal of your product, highlighting its unique features, using persuasive language and keeping it concise, you can create compelling and effective product descriptions that will help you stand out from the competition and make more sales. Remember to use visceral emotional language in your descriptions to invoke feeling in your customers and make them want to buy your products.

Strategies for pricing and shipping

When it comes to pricing and shipping, it can be overwhelming for new Etsy shop owners to figure out the best approach. The pressure of getting it right can cause anxiety and frustration, leaving you feeling like you're constantly second guessing yourself. But fear not, because with the right strategies and a bit of planning, you can confidently price and ship your products to ensure you're making a profit while also keeping your customers happy.

First and foremost, it's important to understand the cost of your products. This includes not just the materials and labor, but also the cost of packaging and shipping. Once you have a clear understanding of these costs, you can begin to determine a fair and competitive price for your products. Keep in mind that pricing too low can devalue your products, while pricing too high can make them unattractive to potential customers. Finding the sweet spot can take some trial and error, but it's worth the effort to get it right.

Another important factor to consider is shipping and handling costs. These can add up quickly, so it's essential to research the most cost-effective shipping options for your products. This may mean finding a balance between speed and cost, or offering free shipping for orders over a certain amount. You can also offer different shipping options for customers to choose from, such as standard or express shipping. By providing multiple options, you can cater to the needs of different customers while also keeping your costs low.

It's also worth considering offering combined shipping for multiple items. This can encourage customers to purchase more than one product, which can increase your sales and reduce shipping costs.

Another strategy to consider is offering free shipping for local customers. This can be an effective way to attract customers who are looking for a more personal touch and also save you money on shipping.

It's also important to keep in mind that shipping and handling costs can vary depending on the location of your customers. It's essential to research the most cost-effective shipping options for international customers as well.

One of the best ways to ensure your pricing and shipping strategies are on point is to keep an eye on your competition. Browse similar products on Etsy and take note of the prices and shipping options they offer. This can give you a better understanding of what's working for others and can help you make informed decisions about your own pricing and shipping strategies.

In conclusion, pricing and shipping can be a daunting task for new Etsy shop owners, but with a bit of planning and research, you can confidently price and ship your products to ensure you're making a profit while also keeping your customers happy. Remember to take into account all your costs and don't be afraid to experiment with different pricing and shipping options to find what works best for your shop.

Chapter 3
Attracting Customers

Attracting customers is one of the most crucial aspects of running a successful Etsy shop. But for new shop owners, the pressure of getting it right can be overwhelming. The thought of having to market your products and build a following can cause feelings of uncertainty and self-doubt. But with the right strategies and a bit of effort, you can confidently attract customers to your store and grow your business.

In this chapter, we'll explore the importance of marketing and how to effectively promote your store. We'll also discuss strategies for building a following and increasing visibility. But before diving into these topics, it's important to understand that attracting customers is a process. It takes time and effort to build a following and establish your brand. But with persistence and the right approach, you can achieve success.

One of the most effective ways to attract customers is through marketing.

This can include a range of tactics, such as social media promotion, email marketing, and influencer partnerships. The key is to find the marketing channels that work best for your store and target audience. For example, if your products are visually appealing, you may want to focus on Instagram and Pinterest to showcase your products. On the other hand, if you sell handmade crafts, you may want to focus on creating a strong presence on Etsy's platform and building relationships with other sellers in your niche.

Another important aspect of attracting customers is building a following. This can be achieved by engaging with your customers, offering excellent customer service, and providing valuable content. For example, you can create a blog or newsletter to share tips and advice related to your products. This can help establish you as an expert in your field and attract customers who are looking for information and inspiration.

Networking and collaborating with other Etsy sellers can also be an effective way to attract customers.

This can include joining groups and communities related to your niche, participating in online forums, and attending craft fairs and events. By building relationships with other sellers, you can gain exposure to new audiences and increase the visibility of your store.

In addition, it's essential to keep an eye on your competition. Browse similar products on Etsy and take note of the strategies they're using to attract customers. This can give you a better understanding of what's working for others and can help you make informed decisions about your own marketing strategies.

In conclusion, attracting customers is a crucial aspect of running a successful Etsy shop. But it can be overwhelming for new shop owners. By understanding the importance of marketing, building a following, and networking, you can confidently attract customers to your store and grow your business. Remember, it's a process, and it takes time and effort, but with persistence and the right approach, you can achieve success.

Importance of marketing and how to promote your store

Marketing is one of the most crucial aspects of running a successful Etsy store. Without effective marketing, even the most beautiful and unique products can get lost in the vast sea of online shops. Your store will be invisible to potential customers and your sales will suffer as a result. But with the right marketing strategy, your store will stand out and attract more customers than you ever thought possible.

Promoting your store is all about making an emotional connection with your customers. You need to connect with them on a visceral level, to make them feel something when they see your products. This is what will make them want to buy from you. One of the best ways to do this is through storytelling. Share the story of how you started your business, what inspired you to create your products, and what you hope to achieve with your store. This will help customers feel a personal connection to your store, and they will be more likely to buy from you.

Another important aspect of marketing is building a community around your store. This can be done through social media, where you can connect with customers and other Etsy sellers. Share your products and your story, and engage with your customers by asking for their opinions and feedback. This will help build trust and loyalty between you and your customers, and they will be more likely to buy from you again in the future.

One of the most powerful marketing tools is word-of-mouth. People trust the opinions of their friends and family more than any other form of advertising. Encourage your customers to share their experiences with your store with their friends and family. This can be done by offering discounts or incentives for referrals, or by simply asking for a review or testimonial.

One of the most effective ways to promote your store is through paid advertising. This can be done through platforms like Google Adwords or Facebook Ads. These platforms allow you to target specific audiences and demographics, so you can reach the customers most likely to buy from your store. This can be a great way to drive traffic to your store and increase sales.

In conclusion, Marketing is a vital aspect of running a successful Etsy store. It's all about making an emotional connection with your customers and building a community around your store. By sharing your story, engaging with your customers, and using paid advertising, you can attract more customers to your store and increase your sales. Remember, the key to a successful Etsy store is to make your customers feel something, and that's what will make them want to buy from you.

Strategies for building a following and increasing visibility

When it comes to building a following and increasing visibility for your Etsy shop, there are several strategies that you can use to make your store stand out and attract more customers. The key is to create a unique and compelling brand that resonates with your target audience. Here are some strategies that you can use to build a following and increase visibility for your Etsy shop.

First, create a strong brand identity. Your brand is the emotional and psychological connection that customers have with your store. It is the combination of your logo, colors, and messaging that create a unique and memorable experience for customers. To create a strong brand identity, you'll want to choose a unique name, logo, and color scheme that are easy to recognize and remember. Additionally, you'll want to create a consistent messaging that speaks to the needs and desires of your target audience.

Second, focus on creating high-quality and visually appealing products. The products that you offer in your Etsy shop are the foundation of your business. To attract customers, you'll need to create products that are visually appealing, high-quality, and unique. Take the time to create detailed and high-quality product photos that showcase your products in the best light possible. Additionally, you'll want to create detailed and compelling product descriptions that speak to the benefits and features of your products.

Third, use social media to promote your store. Social media is a powerful tool that you can use to increase visibility for your Etsy shop. To make the most of social media, you'll want to create a strong presence on platforms like Instagram, Facebook, and Pinterest. Share your products, behind-the-scenes content, and other interesting information about your business. Additionally, use social media to connect with your target audience and build relationships with potential customers.

Fourth, collaborate with other Etsy sellers. Collaborating with other Etsy sellers can be a powerful way to increase visibility for your store. You can participate in joint giveaways, cross-promote your products, or even create a joint collection of products. Additionally, you can collaborate with other Etsy sellers to create a stronger community of like-minded business owners.

Finally, use SEO to increase visibility for your store. SEO, or search engine optimization, is the process of optimizing your online store to rank higher in search engine results. To increase visibility for your store, you'll want to optimize your store's title, tags, and product descriptions for keywords that your target audience is searching for. Additionally, you'll want to focus on creating high-quality backlinks to your store from other websites.

In conclusion, building a following and increasing visibility for your Etsy shop takes time, effort, and dedication. However, by following the strategies outlined above, you can create a unique and compelling brand that resonates with your target audience. You can then use social media, collaborations, SEO, and other strategies to increase visibility for your store and attract more customers. Remember, the key is to build a strong emotional connection with your audience, which will lead to more sales, and more loyal customers.

Tips for networking and collaborating with other Etsy sellers

Networking and collaborating with other Etsy sellers can be a game changer for your online store. It can not only help you to increase your visibility, but also it can help you to gain valuable support, inspiration and valuable tips from the experienced sellers. It's an opportunity to connect with like-minded individuals who understand the challenges of running an Etsy store and can offer valuable advice, resources, and inspiration.

When you collaborate with other sellers, you are not only building relationships, but you're also creating opportunities for cross-promotion, joint ventures, and teaming up on product lines and marketing campaigns. Imagine the feeling of having your products featured on someone else's site or social media channels, reaching a whole new audience of potential customers and bring in more revenue.

Networking and collaborating with other Etsy sellers can

also help you to improve your products, customer service, and overall store. When you connect with other sellers, you can get a fresh perspective on your products, pricing, and customer service. You can learn from others' experiences, avoid common mistakes, and pick up new ideas for your own store.

To begin networking and collaborating with other Etsy sellers, start by joining Etsy Teams. Etsy Teams are groups of Etsy sellers who share a common interest, such as a specific product category or location. Joining a team allows you to connect with other sellers, share advice, and collaborate on promotions and events. You can also join online forums and Facebook groups, where you can connect with other Etsy sellers, ask questions, and share advice.

Another way to network and collaborate with other Etsy sellers is to attend craft fairs and other events. These events provide an opportunity to meet other sellers in person, exchange business cards, and discuss potential collaborations. You can also attend webinars, workshops, and classes, where you can connect with other Etsy sellers, learn new skills, and pick up new ideas.

Networking and collaborating with other Etsy sellers can be an emotional rollercoaster. You might feel overwhelmed and anxious at first, but once you start connecting with other sellers, you'll feel more confident, motivated and empowered. Collaborating with other sellers can be a great way to learn from others, get support, and grow your business. It's a great way to build relationships and gain valuable insights that can help you to improve your store and increase your sales.

In conclusion, networking and collaborating with other Etsy sellers is an essential part of running a successful online store. It can help you to gain visibility, improve your products, and increase your sales. It's an opportunity to connect with like-minded individuals who understand the challenges of running an Etsy store and can offer valuable advice, resources, and inspiration. So, don't be afraid to reach out and start building relationships with other Etsy sellers. The emotional benefits and potential growth for your business are *well worth it.*

Chapter 4
Managing Your Time and Inventory

Managing your time and inventory can be a daunting task, especially for new Etsy shop owners. It's easy to feel overwhelmed by the constant demand to create new products, respond to customer inquiries, and keep up with inventory levels. It can be a never-ending cycle of stress and anxiety, leaving you feeling drained and frustrated. But it doesn't have to be that way.

Effective time management and inventory management are essential for running a successful Etsy store. They are the backbone of your business and can make or break your success. It's important to have a clear understanding of how to manage your time and inventory in order to run a profitable and efficient store.

In this chapter, we will discuss tips and strategies for managing your time and inventory effectively. We'll explore ways to balance multiple tasks, find reliable suppliers, and maintain accurate inventory levels.

We'll also discuss ways to streamline your processes and automate tasks to save time and reduce stress.

One of the keys to effective time management is setting clear and achievable goals. This means setting specific, measurable, attainable, relevant, and time-bound (SMART) goals for your store. By setting clear goals, you can stay focused and motivated, and make sure that you're making the most of your time.

Another key aspect of effective time management is prioritizing your tasks. This means focusing on the most important tasks first and delegating or outsourcing tasks that are not essential to the success of your store. This can help you to stay organized and reduce stress.

When it comes to inventory management, it's important to understand the importance of accurate inventory levels. This means keeping track of your inventory, including product quantities, costs, and reorder dates. It also means understanding your product lifecycle, including product development, production, and distribution. This can help you to plan for future inventory needs and avoid stockouts.

Managing your time and inventory effectively can help you to reduce stress, increase productivity, and grow your business. It can help you to focus on the most important tasks and make the most of your time. It can also help you to maintain accurate inventory levels and plan for future inventory needs. With the right strategies and tools, you can run a profitable and efficient Etsy store.

In this chapter, you will learn how to manage your time and inventory effectively, and you will discover ways to streamline your processes and automate tasks to save time and reduce stress. You will also learn how to set clear and achievable goals, prioritize your tasks, and maintain accurate inventory levels. By the end of this chapter, you will have the tools and knowledge you need to run a profitable and efficient Etsy store, and you will feel more confident, motivated and empowered.

Tips for managing time effectively and balancing multiple tasks

Managing time effectively and balancing multiple tasks can be incredibly challenging, especially when you're just starting out as an Etsy shop owner. The feeling of being overwhelmed and not knowing where to start can be overwhelming and frustrating. But with the right strategies and techniques, you can take control of your time and make your Etsy shop a success.

One of the most important things you can do is to set clear goals for yourself. Determine what you want to accomplish each day, week, and month, and then create a plan to achieve those goals. This will give you a sense of direction and purpose, and help you stay focused on what's important. Next, prioritize your tasks. Not all tasks are created equal, and some are more important than others. Determine which tasks are most critical to the success of your Etsy shop, and make sure to tackle those first.

This will help you stay on track and avoid getting bogged down by less important tasks.

Another key strategy is to break your tasks down into smaller, manageable chunks. Instead of trying to tackle a big project all at once, break it down into smaller steps. This will make it much easier to focus and make progress, and help you avoid feeling overwhelmed.

Additionally, try to automate as many tasks as possible. This can be anything from scheduling social media posts to creating templates for product descriptions. The less time you spend on repetitive tasks, the more time you'll have to focus on the things that truly matter.

Another tip for managing your time effectively is to set regular breaks. Taking regular breaks can help you stay fresh, reduce stress, and increase productivity. Make sure to take a break every hour or so, and use that time to relax, stretch, and clear your mind.

Finally, try to stay organized and keep your work area clean and clutter-free.

A cluttered and disorganized work area can be incredibly distracting and can make it difficult to focus on your tasks. By keeping your work area clean and organized, you'll be able to work more efficiently and avoid feeling overwhelmed.

In conclusion, managing time effectively and balancing multiple tasks can be a daunting task, but with the right strategies and techniques, you can take control of your time and make your Etsy shop a success. With clear goals, prioritization, breaking down tasks, automating, regular breaks and staying organized, you'll be able to stay focused and make steady progress towards your goals. Remember to take care of yourself and give yourself a break when you need it, running an Etsy shop can be emotionally and physically demanding, but with the right approach, it can be an incredibly rewarding experience.

Strategies for finding suppliers and maintaining inventory

When it comes to finding suppliers and maintaining inventory, it can be a daunting and overwhelming task for new Etsy shop owners. The thought of scouring the internet for reliable suppliers and keeping track of inventory can make your head spin and leave you feeling lost and powerless. But with the right strategies and approach, you can easily navigate this crucial aspect of running a successful Etsy shop.

One of the most important things to keep in mind when finding suppliers is to do your research. Don't just jump at the first supplier you come across. Take the time to read reviews and compare prices to ensure that you are getting the best deal. When you find a supplier that you trust and feel comfortable working with, make sure to establish clear communication and set expectations. This will help to prevent any misunderstandings or issues down the line.

Another key strategy for finding suppliers is to diversify your sources. Instead of relying on just one supplier, try to find multiple suppliers for different products.

This will help to ensure that you always have a steady supply of inventory and reduce the risk of stockouts. Additionally, it can also help you to save money by allowing you to shop around for the best deals.

When it comes to maintaining inventory, the key is organization. Create a spreadsheet or use an inventory management software to keep track of your stock levels, reorder points, and sales. This will help you to stay on top of your inventory and ensure that you always have enough product to meet customer demand. Additionally, it will also help you to quickly identify any products that are not selling well, so you can adjust your inventory accordingly.

But perhaps the most challenging aspect of maintaining inventory is keeping your emotions in check. Being a business owner can be stressful, and it's easy to get caught up in the emotional rollercoaster of running a business. It can be frustrating when you receive a low stock notification, or when you have to cancel an order because you don't have enough product. But it's important to remember that these are normal parts of running a business, and they don't define your success as a shop owner.

In conclusion, finding suppliers and maintaining inventory may seem like a daunting task, but with the right strategies and approach, you can easily navigate this crucial aspect of running a successful Etsy shop. Remember to do your research, diversify your sources, stay organized and most importantly, keep your emotions in check. By following these tips, you'll be able to find reliable suppliers, maintain a steady supply of inventory, and create a business that you can be proud of.

Chapter 5
Understanding Legal Requirements

Starting an Etsy shop can be an exciting journey, but it's also a journey that comes with a lot of responsibilities. One of the most important responsibilities is understanding and complying with legal requirements. The thought of navigating the legal landscape of running a business can be overwhelming and nerve-wracking. The fear of not complying with regulations or not knowing what you need to do to stay compliant can make your stomach drop and leave you feeling powerless.

But it's important to remember that understanding legal requirements is not a one-time task. It's an ongoing process that requires constant attention and effort. Failure to comply with legal requirements can lead to serious consequences, such as fines, penalties, and even legal action. So, it's essential to take the time to understand the legal requirements for operating an online store and to create a plan for staying compliant.

In this chapter, we will provide a comprehensive overview of the legal requirements for operating an Etsy shop. We will discuss topics such as taxes, licensing, permits, and regulations. We will also provide tips and resources for staying compliant and avoiding legal issues. By the end of this chapter, you will have a better understanding of the legal requirements for operating an Etsy shop and the tools you need to stay compliant.

One of the most important legal requirements for operating an Etsy shop is paying taxes. As an online business owner, you are responsible for collecting and remitting sales taxes to the appropriate state and local tax authorities. Failure to do so can result in fines and penalties. It's essential to understand the tax laws in your state and to create a plan for collecting and remitting sales taxes.

Another important legal requirement is obtaining the necessary licenses and permits. Depending on the nature of your business, you may need to obtain licenses and permits from your state, county, or city. Failure to obtain the necessary licenses and permits can result in fines and penalties.

Finally, regulations are also an important aspect of operating an Etsy shop. Regulations are rules and guidelines that must be followed to ensure that your business is operating legally and ethically. Regulations can vary depending on the nature of your business and the products you are selling. It's essential to understand and comply with regulations to avoid legal issues.

In conclusion, understanding legal requirements is a crucial aspect of running a successful Etsy shop. Failure to comply with legal requirements can lead to serious consequences, such as fines, penalties, and even legal action. This chapter aims to provide a comprehensive overview of the legal requirements for operating an Etsy shop and to provide tips and resources for staying compliant and avoiding legal issues. Remember, it's better to be safe than sorry, and by understanding legal requirements and staying compliant, you *can focus on growing your business with peace of mind.*

Overview of legal requirements for operating an online store

Operating an online store can be a daunting task, especially when it comes to understanding and complying with legal requirements. The thought of navigating the complex world of taxes and regulations can be overwhelming and leave you feeling anxious and stressed. However, it is essential to stay compliant and avoid costly penalties. In this article, we will provide an overview of legal requirements for operating an online store to help ease your worries and give you a better understanding of what is expected of you.

One of the most important legal requirements for operating an online store is to obtain the necessary licenses and permits. Depending on your location and the products you are selling, you may need to apply for a sales tax permit, business license, or other forms of authorization. Failure to obtain these can lead to hefty fines and penalties, leaving you feeling helpless and defeated.

Another crucial legal requirement is to comply with consumer protection laws. As an online store owner, you have a legal obligation to protect the privacy of your customers and provide accurate information about your products. This includes ensuring that your website is secure, using clear and concise language in your product descriptions, and providing a clear refund and exchange policy. Failing to comply with consumer protection laws can lead to legal action and damage to your reputation, causing you to lose customers and revenue.

In addition to the above, it is also essential to comply with product safety regulations. As an online store owner, you are responsible for ensuring that your products are safe for use and meet the necessary standards. This includes providing clear and accurate product information, such as ingredients, warnings, and instructions. Failure to comply with product safety regulations can lead to recalls and legal action, leaving you feeling like your business is crumbling before your eyes. Furthermore, as an online store owner, you also need to be aware of intellectual property rights. This includes ensuring that you have the necessary licenses and permissions to use any images or content on your website. Using copyrighted material without permission can lead to legal action and costly fines, leaving you feeling like you've been robbed of your hard-earned money.

In conclusion, operating an online store comes with a lot of legal requirements that can be overwhelming and stressful. However, with a little research and understanding, you can stay compliant and avoid costly penalties. Make sure to obtain the necessary licenses and permits, comply with consumer protection laws, product safety regulations, and intellectual property rights. By taking the time to understand and comply with legal requirements, you can run your online store with confidence and avoid the feeling of being stuck in a legal nightmare.

Tips for complying with taxes and regulations

Complying with taxes and regulations can be a daunting and overwhelming task for new Etsy shop owners. The thought of navigating the complex world of taxes and regulations can make your stomach turn, your palms sweat and your heart race. It's important to understand that while this process may be intimidating, it is essential to the success and longevity of your Etsy shop.

The first step in complying with taxes and regulations is to obtain a sales tax permit. This permit allows you to collect and remit sales tax to the appropriate state or local government. Failure to obtain a permit and pay sales tax can result in penalties and fines. It can also lead to the closure of your Etsy shop, leaving you devastated and heartbroken.

Next, it is important to understand and comply with any laws and regulations regarding the products you are selling. For example, if you are selling food items, you will need to comply with food safety regulations.

. If you are selling handmade items, you will need to comply with labor laws and ensure that your products are made in a safe and ethical manner. Ignoring these laws and regulations can lead to legal action against you and your Etsy shop, which can be devastating and financially ruinous.

Another important aspect of complying with taxes and regulations is keeping accurate and detailed records. This includes keeping records of all sales, expenses, and inventory. These records will be necessary when it comes time to file your taxes. Failure to keep accurate records can lead to problems with the IRS and state tax authorities, which can be a nightmare.

It's also important to be aware of any taxes and regulations specific to your state or municipality. For example, some states have laws that require online sellers to collect and remit sales tax, while others do not. It's essential to know what laws apply to you and your Etsy shop so that you can comply with them and avoid any legal issues.

It's clear that complying with taxes and regulations can be a daunting and overwhelming task for new Etsy shop owners. However, it's essential to the success and longevity of your Etsy shop. By obtaining a sales tax permit, understanding and complying with laws and regulations, keeping accurate records, and being aware of state and local laws, you can ensure that your Etsy shop is compliant and avoid any legal issues.

In conclusion, following the laws and regulations can be a challenging task, but it's a necessary step to ensure your Etsy shop runs smoothly and last long. It's important to take the time to understand the laws and regulations that apply to your shop and to consult with professionals if you have any questions. Remember, compliance is key to the success of your Etsy shop, and it's worth the effort to ensure that you are operating within the law.

Conclusion

As you reach the conclusion of this book, it's likely that you're feeling a mix of emotions. You may be feeling proud of all that you've accomplished in setting up and managing your Etsy shop, but also overwhelmed by all of the information and tasks that you've had to navigate. It's understandable to feel a sense of relief that you've made it this far, but also a lingering uncertainty about what lies ahead.

Starting an Etsy shop is a big step, and it's not uncommon to have moments of self-doubt and uncertainty. But it's important to remember that you've come a long way since you first began this journey. You've learned about the Etsy platform, how to optimize your online store, how to attract customers, and how to manage your time and inventory.

You've also learned about the importance of complying with taxes and regulations, a crucial step in operating a successful Etsy shop.

As you look back on all that you've accomplished, it's natural to feel a sense of accomplishment and pride.

You've taken the initiative to start your own business, and that's no small feat. You've also put in the hard work and effort to make it a success. You should be proud of all that you've achieved, and the confidence that you've gained along the way.

However, it's important to remember that starting an Etsy shop is not a one-time event. It's an ongoing process that requires constant effort and attention. You'll need to continue to market and promote your store, create new products, and manage your time and inventory. You'll also need to stay up-to-date on laws and regulations and make sure you're always in compliance.

But don't let this discourage you. Remember, you've already come so far, and you've got what it takes to continue on this journey. You've got the knowledge, the skills, and the determination to make your Etsy shop a success. And with the right mindset and approach, you'll be able to overcome any challenges that come your way.

In conclusion, starting an Etsy shop is a big step and

requires a lot of effort, but it's also a fulfilling and rewarding experience. The journey may be tough, but it's essential to remember that you've accomplished a lot and you're capable of continuing the journey. You should be proud of your achievements and embrace the uncertainty of the future with confidence and determination, knowing that you have the knowledge, skills and mindset to make your Etsy shop a success.

Summary of key points covered in the book

Starting an Etsy shop can be a daunting task, especially for beginners who may not have experience with e-commerce or online sales. But with the right knowledge and tools, anyone can build a successful online store. In this book, we've covered the key points that beginners need to know to understand the Etsy platform and set up an online store.

First, we delved into the world of the Etsy platform, providing an in-depth overview of its features and tools. We showed beginners how to set up an account and create a shop, and how to navigate the interface with ease. We aimed to empower beginners with the knowledge they need to confidently navigate the Etsy platform and make the most of its features.

Next, we focused on optimizing the online store. We stressed the importance of high-quality product photography and provided tips on how to take professional-looking photos.We also provided strategies for creating effective product descriptions and pricing products competitively. Our goal was to help beginners create an online store that is both attractive and user-friendly, one that customers would want to visit and purchase from.

We also covered how to attract customers to the store, which is a crucial aspect of any online business. We discussed the importance of marketing and provided strategies for promoting the store and building a following. We also shared tips on networking and collaborating with other Etsy sellers, which can help beginners increase their visibility and attract more customers. Our aim was to help beginners build a loyal customer base that would keep coming back for more.

Managing time and inventory is also an important aspect of running an online store. We provided tips on how to manage time effectively and balance multiple tasks. We also discussed strategies for finding reliable suppliers and maintaining inventory. Our goal was to help beginners manage their time and inventory efficiently, so they can focus on growing their business.

Finally, we covered the legal requirements for operating an online store. We provided an overview of taxes and regulations that beginners need to comply with, and we shared tips on how to do so. Our aim was to help beginners understand and comply with legal requirements, so they can operate their Etsy shop with confidence and peace of mind.

In summary, this book has provided beginners with the knowledge and tools they need to understand the Etsy platform and set up a successful online store. We've covered everything from setting up an account and creating a shop, to optimizing the online store, attracting customers, managing time and inventory, and complying with legal requirements. With this information, beginners can confidently start and manage an Etsy shop and turn their passion into a thriving business.

Resources for further learning and support

Starting an Etsy shop can be a daunting task, especially for beginners who may not have experience with e-commerce or online sales. The process can be overwhelming, and it's easy to feel lost and alone. However, there are many resources available to help you succeed. These resources can provide you with the support and guidance you need to navigate the Etsy platform, create a successful online store, and attract customers.

One of the most valuable resources for Etsy beginners is the Etsy community. This community is made up of other Etsy sellers, who can provide you with valuable tips and advice. They can share their experiences and help you avoid common mistakes. They can also offer support and encouragement when you're feeling overwhelmed. Joining online groups and forums for Etsy sellers can be a great way to connect with other sellers and learn from their experiences.

Another valuable resource is the Etsy blog and help center.

The blog is a great source of information on a variety of topics related to Etsy, including how to set up and optimize your shop,how to market your products, and how to stay compliant with legal requirements. The help center is a comprehensive resource that provides answers to common questions and guides you through the process of setting up and managing your shop. This will help you avoid a lot of the common mistakes and challenges that beginners face when they're starting an Etsy shop.

Another important resource is the Etsy webinars and educational videos. These webinars provide valuable information on a variety of topics, including how to create a successful online store, how to market your products, and how to stay compliant with legal requirements. The videos are a great way to learn about the Etsy platform and its features, as well as tips and strategies for creating a successful online store. These resources can provide you with the knowledge and skills you need to navigate the Etsy platform and create a successful online store.

In addition to these resources, there are also many books and courses available that can help you succeed on Etsy. These books and courses are written by experienced Etsy sellers and provide valuable information on a variety of topics, including how to set up and optimize your shop, how to market your products, and how to stay compliant with legal requirements. These resources can provide you with the knowledge and skills you need to navigate the Etsy platform and create a successful online store.

Starting an Etsy shop can be a challenging and emotional journey, but it doesn't have to be. With the right resources and support, you can navigate the Etsy platform, create a successful online store, and attract customers. The resources available to you can help you overcome the obstacles that beginners face when they're starting an Etsy shop. With the right resources and support, you can turn your dream of starting an Etsy shop into a reality.

In conclusion, starting an Etsy shop can be a challenging and emotional journey, but it doesn't have to be. The Etsy community, the Etsy blog and help center, Etsy webinars and educational videos, books, and courses are all valuable resources that can provide you with the support and guidance you need to navigate the Etsy platform and create a successful online store. With the right resources and support, you can turn your dream of starting an Etsy shop into a reality. Don't let fear and uncertainty hold you back, take the first step and reach out for help, and you'll be surprised how much you can achieve.